COME & PLAY

♪ ♪ ♪ ♪
Haru koro no hana no en
♪ ♪ ♪ ♪
Meguru sakazuki kage sashite
♪ ♪ ♪

♪ Chiyo no matsu ga ♪ e wake ideshi
♪
♪ Mukashi ♪ no ♪ hikari Ima izu ko

Vikram walks into a bar with a duck on his head . . .

-- and the duck says, "I don't know, I just got here!"

BWA-HA-HA!

Always joking! Men do not marry silly girls!

Is that...?

What **is** she making!?!

Dig a circle there. Make it big!

Goof, it's almost 9:30. Gotta open the shop.

I'll do it!

Okay, but I gotta take the store's wet suit with me.

Some other time?

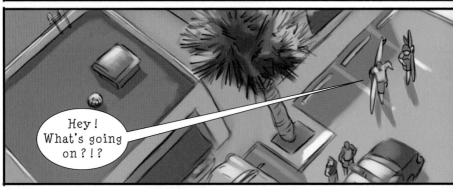

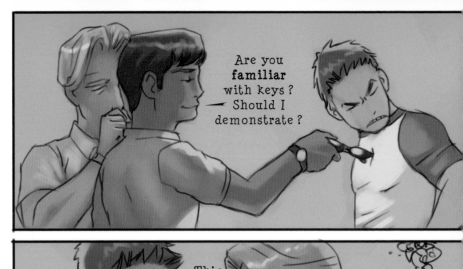

Yeah.
He called it
in.

Saw a guy
messing with
the back door.

Might
wanna replace
that lock.

C'mon, Goof.
Let's go finish your
sand castles.

Yeah,
wuddup
widdat?
You
gonna
regress
to
fashion
dolls
next?

Just
felt
like
making
some
sand
castles
today...

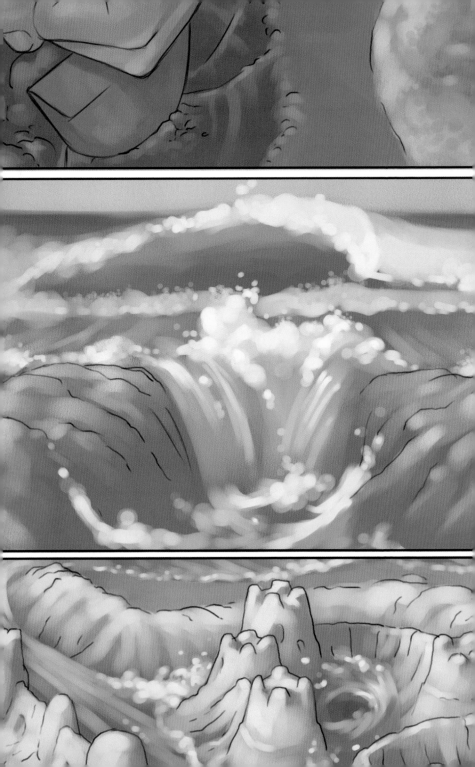

Whew! Can we take a break? I'm dying.

HONK!
HONK!

I've got a delivery for you guys.

Us ?!?

Well, you're "the kids playing volleyball near SunRay's."

Who sent it?

Doesn't say.

Energy drinks ?!?!?

Should we drink this? Maybe it's from some maniac.

Relax, it's safe.

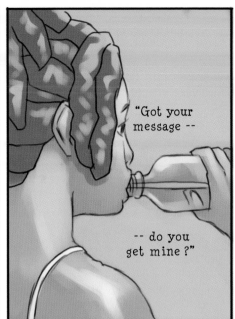

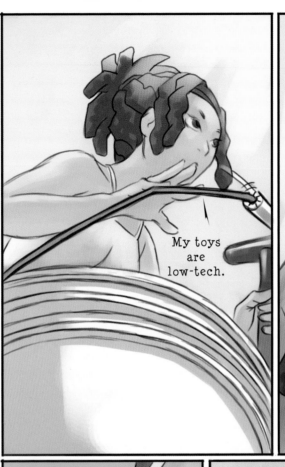

My toys
are
low-tech.

And
harmless.

I
thought you
only used your
powers for
good.

So now I'm
a bad guy?

Are you?

Is your **boyfriend** in trouble now?

Ah. We have a motive.

I know the Price family. I thought their shop was being burgled.

It was Scott's first official surfing instructor gig. He works there.

Not for long, if I know Ray.

Coffee?

So... what happened?

Scott left the door unlocked.

And those other guys?

And how do **you** know this lovely lady?

We're engaged.

She promises to tell me her name after the wedding.

HA!

Oh, well, as best man, allow me...

Zip Carlisle, your bride, Suki Lieber.

Char!
It's
yours!

Foul
again!!!

WHAT
?!?
Foul?!?

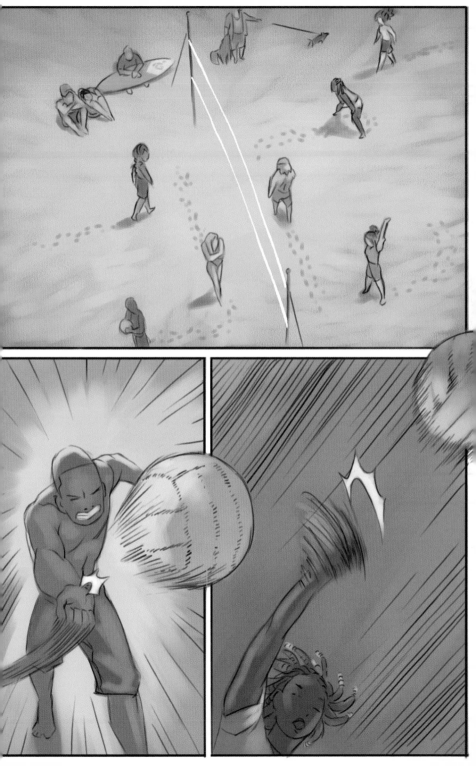

Think you can stand?

Yeah. I'm okay.

WHERE'S FIFI?

If you mean your friends, they left.

Well ... it's a good thing she left ...

Yes, a very good thing!

You saw my bump.

A flawless forearm pass, I'll admit.

Why do you play with weak team mates?

I asked them to. They're my friends...

They're rather mediocre.

They know. Do **you** know you have an accent?

Getting anywhere with Ray Price yet, Char?

henh henh henh

It's true Ray is very handsome, but --

Pooja, Ray is **TOTALLY HOT**.

He's got "cad" written all over him.

BW AHAHAHA!

"Cad"? Pooch, you are **so** cute.

My English . . . is there a better word?

Cad's an excellent word.

I'm just not sure it applies to Ray.

It was New Year's Eve, four years ago.

Hi!
It's nice to
meet --

Yeah.
Uh huh.

And I
thought, "What
a **jerk**!"

"Jerk"

-- is
that a
better
word?

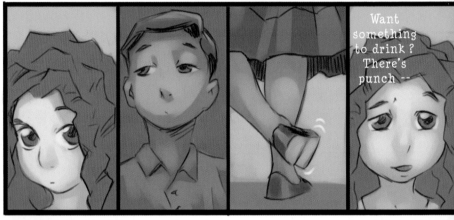

Hey,
why don't you
get us both a
soda.

Um,
okay.
Be right
back.

Wanna
watch this
with me?

What
is
it?

New Year's show.
Lotta good
bands.

N'Sync?

Oh, yeah. I think
they're coming
right up.

So, your name's Suki?
What grade are you in?

8th.

I'm in 9th.

You're new
here.

Moved from
Ohio a few
weeks ago.
You going out
with anyone?

. . . no . . .

Ever
been
kissed?

Not . . .
really . . .

He was sooo0000000000 gorgeous.

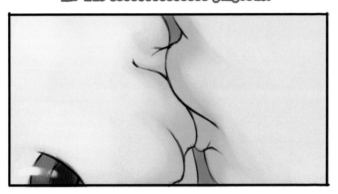

YOU NEVER TOLD ME THIS !!!

He kissed you ?!? In your bedroom ?!? Mm-hmm...

Details, girl! DETAILS!

It was amazing.

Now you've really been kissed.

Beyonce

Kids! Join us! The ball's about to drop!

We go in with the adults like nothing's happened.

Later...

See you at school?

So! Need help finding your way around?

I'll manage.

When I first came here, I was so --

Spence! Save me a seat!

I . . .
I was
so . . .

Shhhh! Let's not disturb people.

Ooooookay! =tee-hee=

Zach, what's the matter? Are you in trouble?

...uh ...is Char here?

Uh-huh... aaaaand Pooja.

Knock it off, Suki. Listen...

Hiiiiiiiiiii, Suki!

...ע...

"Oy"
is right...

Isn't your brother
the sweetest ?

I
lost
my
keys
at
the
club...

Char's
dad...?

Outta town and Char
turned off her phone.

Speaking
of Char...

Why is she here?

I should have left her at the club?

Suki always brings home people who need help.

But not Beau DuGray's fiancé...

Big bad Beau won't be back until tomorrow morning...

I'm **NOT** taking that bimbette home!

Do you have a bathroom...?

This way, dear.

Chardonnay, would you please lend Randi your house key so --

I'm afraid she's in no condition to go anywhere tonight.

...doan feel so good...

You'll feel better in the morning, dear.

...not when Beau finds out...

Jack, Lewis, and I were at the Boho when we heard a ruckus.

Randi was drunk, dancing on a table.

It starts with an INNOCENT QUESTION...

...that leads to a CHALLENGE...

...that becomes an OBSESSION...

...and finally EXPLODES in ANGER!

It's

LIFE ! CAMERA ! ACTION !

starring
Serenity !

While "Life!" goes on, everybody's favorite
blue-haired oddball and her friends turn their
energy and talents behind the "Camera!" to make
"Action!" movies with a decidedly different perspective!

Coming Soon from Thomas Nelson and Realbuzz Studios -
four BRAND NEW Serenity stories!

Serenity Vol. 7
Space Cadet vs. Drama Queen

Serenity Vol. 8
Sunday Best

Serenity Vol. 9
Choosing Change

Serenity Vol. 10
Girl Overboard

...and
featuring
these
"movies"!

For more info visit
www.SerenityBuzz.com
www.RealbuzzStudios.com

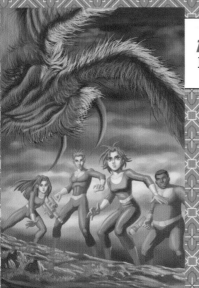

TERROR FROM THE TARANTULA NEBULA
Deep space voyagers discover a sinister secret!

CRAWLING FROM THE WRECKAGE
All exits blocked!
Earthquake at the mall!

ESTHER, QUEEN OF PERSIA
A Biblical epic of romance and intrigue!

FRAULEIN STEIN'S MONSTER
Monster mayhem marks a remarkable revelation!

Hey, folks! They're not really "movies" - they're stories that READ like movies!

THE revolve TOUR

Hawk Nelson

Natalie Grant

KJ-52

ALL NEW EVENT for Teen Girls
PRESENTED BY WOMEN OF FAITH

Max & Jenna Lucado

Ayiesha Woods

We're Coming to a City Near You!
TOUR DATES

Columbus, OH
September 14 - 15, 2007

Dallas, TX
September 21 - 22, 2007

Hartford, CT
September 28 - 29, 2007

St. Louis, MO
October 5 - 6, 2007

Anaheim, CA
October 12 - 13, 2007

Sacramento, CA
October 19 - 20, 2007

Philadelphia, PA
November 2 - 3, 2007

Minneapolis, MN
November 9 - 10, 2007

Portland, OR
November 16 - 17, 2007

Atlanta, GA
November 30 - Dec. 1, 2007

Orlando, FL
January 25 - 26, 2008

Charlotte, NC
February 1 - 2, 2008

Denver, CO
February 15 - 16, 2008

Houston, TX
February 22 - 23, 2008

Chad Eastham

Kimiko Soldati

Download **Preview Video** Online

To register by phone, call 877-9-REVOLVE
or online at REVOLVETOUR.COM

Dates, locations and guests are subject to change.
The Revolve Tour is produced by Women of Faith, Inc. Women of Faith is a ministry division of Thomas Nelson Publishers.

Goofyfoot Gurl

Hot Dogger: Tony Weinstock
Wahine: Allison Barrows
Big kahuna: Realbuzz Studios
Shakas To: Allen A., Amanda B,
Jennifer D., & all our new friends at Thomas N.!

Published by Thomas Nelson, Inc. Nashville, TN 37214 www.thomasnelson.com

Library of Congress Cataloguing-in-Publication Data
Applied For

Scripture quotations marked NCV are taken from
The Holy Bible, New Century Version®. NCV®.
Copyright © 2001 by Nelson Bibles.
Used by permission of Thomas Nelson. All rights reserved.

Printed in Singapore.
5 4 3 2 1

VISIT GOOFYFOOT GURL AT:
www.RealbuzzStudios.com